BLESS THE DAY

ALSO BY JUNE COTNER

*Bedside Prayers: Prayers & Poems for When You Rise
and Go to Sleep*

*Graces: Prayers & Poems for Everyday Meals
and Special Occasions*

*The Home Design Handbook: The Essential Planning
Guide for Building, Buying, or Remodeling a Home*

*Heal Your Soul, Heal the World: Prayers and Poems to
Comfort, Inspire, and Connect Humanity*

BLESS THE DAY

PRAYERS & POEMS TO NURTURE YOUR SOUL

JUNE COTNER

Kodansha International

NEW YORK • TOKYO • LONDON

Kodansha America, Inc.
114 Fifth Avenue, New York, New York 10011, U.S.A.

Kodansha International Ltd.
17-14 Otowa 1-chome, Bunkyo-ku, Tokyo 112-8652, Japan

Published in 1998 by Kodansha America, Inc.

Copyright © by June Cotner Graves
All rights reserved.

Library of Congress Cataloging-in-Publication Data
Cotner, June, 1950–
    Bless the day : prayers and poems to nurture your soul / June
Cotner
        p.   cm.
    Includes index.
    ISBN 1-56836-251-X
    1. Christian poetry. 2. Spiritual life—Poetry. I. Title.
PS595.C47C59   1998
811.008'03823—dc21   98-21401   CIP

Book design by Jessica Shatan

Manufactured in the United States of America

98 99 00 01 02 QFF   10 9 8 7 6 5 4 3 2 1

This book is dedicated to

my mother,
BETTY ELVIRA BAXTER
(1925–1961)

my grandfather,
RUSSELL PORTER BAXTER
(1897–1967)

and my uncle,
ALBERT EDWARD BAXTER
(1923–1996)

*Your heart has brought
great joy to many. Those hearts
can never forget you.*

Flavia Weeden

CONTENTS

Contents

xiv

A Letter to Readers

BLESS THE DAY GREW OUT OF A DESIRE TO create a book of spiritual poems and prayers that celebrated life's daily blessings. The poems I found and the submissions I accepted seemed to fall into themes such as love, faith, courage, healing, and wonder. While some of the themes seem more positive than others (e.g., love vs. healing), I feel that at various times in our lives we need the "blessings" of faith, courage, and healing every bit as much as the satisfaction that love, joy, and wonder can bring to our lives.

Most, if not all, of the poets represented in the book have learned to find the spark of divinity in the challenging, and sometimes tragic, events that befall all of us at one time or another. For example, the selection on page 128, "For What We Have Today," was written by Lillian J. Loyd, a mother whose son drowned at age sixteen. The poem is a reflection of her young son's words, which have given her much comfort and inspiration through the years.

Many of the blessings can be read during specific life passages such as weddings, anniversaries, christenings, birthdays, funerals, and graduations. I am especially drawn to the following thought by David Steindel-Rast:

To bless whatever there is,
and for no other reason but simply because it is,
that is what we are made for as human beings.

A subject index on page 193 offers my recommendations for special events. All of the blessings here can be used anytime you need a spirit lifted, a heart comforted, or a thought embraced. But the subject index will give you ideas for blessing that special moment, whether it's a graduation, memorial service, or wedding. Another way in which this book can be used is to copy a favorite selection on a blank greeting card and send it to a friend or relative. Please be sure to credit the poet.

My two previous anthologies, *Graces* and *Bedside Prayers*, as well as the book you're now holding, reflect a balance of approximately twenty percent classic and famous authors (for familiarity) and eighty percent contemporary poets (for freshness). One of the goals in my anthologies is to create a platform for relatively unknown poets to receive the recognition they deserve. In *Bless the Day*, I believe you'll come to appreciate the poetry of the unknown or lesser-known poets every bit as much as that of the famous writers.

I love spiritual poetry and will continue to compile anthologies that move me and hopefully enrich all of our lives. If you come across a special poem you think I would enjoy, or want to share a few of your own spiritual poems, please send them to me at the address below. Typed copies are always appreciated (with your name, address, and phone number at the top of each page). If you include a self-addressed stamped envelope, you'll eventually receive a reply. I hope to hear from you!

JUNE COTNER
P.O. Box 2765
Poulsbo, WA 98370

THANKS

As THE COMPILER AND EDITOR OF *BLESS THE Day*, I feel this book is written through me rather than by me. It's the product of many people, both living and dead. I feel honored to have found myself as essentially the conduit for so many beautiful poems to be published.

The living poets who submitted for this book, as well as the poets who are no longer with us, all leave an indelible trace of wonder, beauty, and poignancy in our world. They are the souls who are gifted with the ability to translate spiritual experiences into a language that speaks to everyone.

In my daily life I am still stunned by and find myself in awe of the synchronicity that brings me—circuitously at times—to possible selections for my books, whether it's an obscure poem in a long-out-of-print book, a phrase I happen to hear at a lecture, something broadcast over the radio, or a statement on a television program. When I discover such a gem, my smile says, "Thank you, God." Life's blessings, indeed, surround us every day.

Strangers have offered their kindness as well. After reading *Graces*, Kaia L. Lenhart sent me the selection on page 89, "No One Walks Alone," and Ruth Fee sent me the selection on page 94, "Father Forgive." Just before the final manuscript for *Bless the Day* was completed, Paula Vayas sent me her favorite prayer by Thomas Merton, "Trust," on page 25.

Many dear friends, relatives, and award-winning poets have become part of the process of honing a too-long "test market" manuscript into a succinct and highly readable book. In particular, I wish to thank my husband, Jim Graves, my sister, Sue Cotner, my daughter, Kirsten Cotner Myrvang, and my cousin, Margie Cotner Potts.

The friends who critiqued my two previous books, *Graces* and *Bedside Prayers*, and who were delighted to offer feedback on *Bless the Day*, are Arnie Anfinson, Sue Gitch, Fern Halgren, Susan Peterson, and Sandra Van Ausdal.

I would also like to thank my friends Lynn Eathorne Bradley, Deborah Ham, and Patricia Huckell, wonderful supporters of my anthologies who kindly agreed to critique this book.

The process of compiling anthologies has brought new friends into my life. Many thanks to Father Paul Keenan (author of *Good News for Bad Days* and host of the national ABC radio program *Religion on the Line*) for critiquing the manuscript and bringing more joy to my life with laughter and insights. In many ways, Father Paul feels like the brother I never had. I am also grateful to Jack Canfield (coauthor of *Chicken Soup for the Soul*) for both his encouragement of my work and enthusiastic endorsement of my anthologies.

Helping out in the word processing department were Kim Langevin and my son Kyle Myrvang. In the eleventh hour of churning out the test market manuscript, Suzie Long came to the rescue. I'd also like to thank Kevin Jennings for providing excellent computer assistance, and Tricia Treacy for her help in securing permissions.

My life has been so blessed and enriched by the many poets who contributed to this book, as well as by the many excellent poets who didn't make the final cut due to the ultimate length of the book. In particular, I'm especially grateful to the following contributing poets who went "above and beyond the call" to critique the manuscript and help transform *Bless the Day* into the book it became: poetry anthologist Meg Campbell, Barbara Crooker (winner of many poetry awards), Penny Harter (author of *Turtle Blessing, Lizard Light: Poems from the Earth*, and thirteen other books), Shirley Kobar (published in the anthologies *Between the Heartbeats* and *Bedside Prayers*), Elizabeth Searle Lamb (author of *Today and Every Day*), Arlene Gay Levine (author of *39 Ways to Open Your Heart*), and Jo-Anne Rowley (contributor to *Graces* and *Bedside Prayers*).

I know *Bless the Day* would not have become what it is without the encouragement and input of my editor, Nancy Cooperman Su, at Kodansha. Deepest thanks go to Nancy for seeing and appreciating the vision for *Bless the Day* from the sample pages submitted with the book proposal. Along with the other critiquers, Nancy also spent considerable time evaluating the test market manuscript. Nancy, it's been delightful working with you!

My heartfelt gratitude goes to my agent, Denise Marcil. I've had the pleasure of knowing Denise for nearly a decade now. In addition to shepherding five of my ideas into published books so expertly, she's been a dear friend as well. Denise is someone I can count on to represent my books with the utmost integrity. She's honest, responsive, and truly the best businessperson I know.

And lastly, I'm deeply grateful to the Creator who guides us to become all we can, who comforts us during our setbacks and disappointments, and who rejoices with us in the blessings we find along the way.

LOVE

To Love Another

For one human being to love another human
being: that is perhaps the most difficult task that
has been entrusted to us, the ultimate task, the
final test and proof, the work for which all other
work is merely preparation. Loving does not at
first mean merging, surrendering, and uniting
with another person—it is a high inducement for
the individual to ripen, to become something in
himself, to become world in himself for the sake
of another person; it is a great, demanding claim
on him, something that chooses him and calls him
to vast distances.

RAINER MARIA RILKE
(1875–1926)
Translated by Stephen Mitchell

With Great Love

We can do no great things,
Only small things with great love.

MOTHER TERESA
(1910-1997)

Love

4

Paiute Wedding Prayer

Now you will feel no rain,
For each of you will be shelter to the other.
Now you will feel no cold,
For each of you will be warmth to the other.
Now there is no more loneliness.
Now you are two persons,
But there is only one life before you.
Go now to your dwelling place,
To enter into the days of your togetherness,
And may your days be good and long upon this
      earth.

AUTHOR UNKNOWN

Love

Song

Love that is hoarded, moulds at last
Until we know some day
The only thing we ever have
Is what we give away.

And kindness that is never used
But hidden all alone
Will slowly harden till it is
As hard as any stone.

It is the things we always hold
That we will lose some day;
The only things we ever keep
Are what we give away.

HAROLD C. SANDALL

Love

6

It's All I Have to Bring To-day

It's all I have to bring to-day
This, and my heart beside,
This and my heart, and all the fields,
And all the meadows wide.
Be sure you count, should I forget,—
Some one the sum could tell,—
This and my heart, and all the bees
Which in the clover dwell.

EMILY DICKINSON
(1830–1886)

Wedding Prayer

Lord, give us the strength to walk hand in hand,
in step with each other, the rest of our days.
Never take from us the gift of your love,
for which we are thankful, in so many ways.
We pledge, Lord, to honor
this commitment we make,
to ourselves and to you,
with the help of your grace.
Please send us your blessing on this happy day,
may our joy at this wedding be never erased.

NOREEN BRAMAN

Loving

God . . . help me to believe
That it is never late
To hope, to pray . . . for love.

Yet, as I wait for that
            special one,
Grant me the grace, the heart,
To reach toward others
With a love like Yours;
Others, who may be lonely,
            waiting, too . . .
For all are one, in You.

Thus, waiting, I will have found
            love still–
Oh, not in the eyes of One . . .
            but Many.

WILLIAM DEERFIELD

Love Is Patient

Love is patient, love is kind.
It does not envy, it does not boast,
it is not proud. It is not rude,
it is not self-seeking,
it is not easily angered,
it keeps no records of wrongs.

Love does not delight in evil
but rejoices with the truth.
It always protects, always trusts,
always hopes, always preserves.
Love never fails.

And now these three remain:
faith, hope and love.

But the greatest of these is love.

I Corinthians 13:4–13

The Bear That Came to the Wedding

In this poem the Bear shambles in
   like a slightly drunken uncle,
politely hands the Bride
   a tidy knot of Shooting Star, Strawberry
Blossoms, and Violets, nips
   the Groom gently on the left shank
and disappears, humming or snorting
   we are not sure, but dancing
certainly, and we are left alone
   with the enormity of the forest's blessing,
wondering what to make of our lives after this,
   the Bear's visit, thinking it might mean
             Love.

HOWARD McCORD

Love Much

Love much. Earth has enough of bitter in it;
  Cast sweets into its cup whene'er you can.
No heart so hard but love at last may win it.
    Yes, love on through doubt and darkness, and
    believe
There is no thing which love may not achieve.

ELLA WHEELER WILCOX
(1850–1919)

Airborne

My mother, 72,
turns to the handsome man seated beside
her on the plane.
"I bet you were hoping to sit next to
an attractive young blonde."
Smiling, he replies, "I am."

MEG CAMPBELL

For the Children

Bless the children
Of the world.
May each child have
A mother's love
And father's strength,
Milk to make strong bones
And honey to taste life's sweetness.

May each have shelter from the cold,
Laughter to warm the heart,
Freedom to grow to potential
And knowledge of Your love.

JO-ANNE ROWLEY

Love

14

The Life of Love

May I so live the life of love
this day that all those with whom I have
anything to do may be as sure of love
in the world as they are of the sunlight.

AUTHOR UNKNOWN

The Human Touch

'Tis the human touch in this world that counts,
The touch of your hand and mine,
Which means far more to the fainting heart
Than shelter and bread and wine;
For shelter is gone when the night is o'er,
And bread lasts only a day,
But the touch of the hand and the sound of the
voice
Sings on in the soul always.

SPENCER MICHAEL FREE

Now the Heart

Years from now the heart
Will bear out its journey
And retain the magic
It is always learning.

Years from now the heart
Will listen to silence
And hear reverberations
Deep inside the earth.

The heart will trust itself
To heal, and, when in doubt,
To trace the perimeter
Of its own brilliant soul.

Years from now the heart
Will exist as the perfect
Point of entry for all
The lightness of this world.

Love

CORRINE DE WINTER

Water's Prayer

Leafless aspens groom
the iced breeze, while below

a brook descends the mountain
with its musical story, remembering

the serenity of sky, and lightning's clear passion.
Water knows what is far will be near.

Water says choose that which closes distance,
choose touch. When snow falls,

and a green mystery is carried
by all that moves,

choose love.

JAMES BERTOLINO

Love

18

FAITH

Starry Field

I was sunk into darkness
    and you lifted me to Light.
The ground was pulled from under me.
    You picked me up
    and set me again in your starry field.
I was weary. My eyes closed.
    You opened them
    and made me look.
My ears heard only laughter,
noise, and confusion.
    You sang a simple song,
    for the infant unable
    to make known its smallest need and said:
            "Let us begin."

I am beginning again.

JULIA OLDER

Faith

21

On Wings of Air

To have Faith—
in the best and highest that we know—
is to be borne along,
through the difficulties of life—
as on wings of air.

AUTHOR UNKNOWN

Faith

Angel Embrace

There are angels who sit quietly
and whisper when we need comfort.
There are those who breathe life into us
when we are breathless.

There are angels who fill us with gracious support
when our souls become fragile,
and those who kiss us goodnight for a peaceful
    slumber.

There are angels that touch us with sacred
    laughter
when tears become a burden.
There are those who wrap their wings around us
and rock us until the ache in our heart disappears.

There are angels that can send us flying with
    wonder
when our hope begins to fade,
and those who devote everything to give us
everlasting peace in heaven.

LORI EBERHARDY

I Have Lost My Way

I have been apart and I have lost my way. . . .
And in my hours of darkness
    when I am not even sure
there is a Thou hearing my call,
I still call to Thee with all my heart.
Hear the cry of my voice,
    clamoring from this desert,
for my soul is parched and my heart can barely
    stand this longing.

Gnostic Holy Eucharist

Faith

24

Trust

My Lord God, I have no idea where I'm going,
I do not see the road ahead of me.
I cannot know for certain where it will end.
Nor do I really know myself, and the fact that I think
    that I am following your will does not mean that
    I am actually doing so.
But I believe that the desire to please you
    does in fact please you.
And I hope I have that desire in all that I am doing.
I hope that I will never do anything
    apart from that desire.
And I know that if I do this
    you will lead me by the right road
    though I may know nothing about it.
Therefore I will trust you always though I may seem
to be lost in the shadow of death.
I will not fear, for you are ever with me,
and you will never leave me to face my perils alone.

THOMAS MERTON
(1915–1968)

Faith

God's Way

Learn that the silence
Is God's way of pausing
So that we may hear
The voice of faith.

CORRINE DE WINTER

Keep This for Me

"Keep this for me."
What child has not said this,
And placed a treasure in his mother's hand
With strict injunction she should keep it safe
Till he return?
He knows with her it will be safe;
No troubled thought or anxious fear besets his
    mind,
And off he runs lighthearted to his play.

If children can so trust, why cannot we,
And place our treasures, too, in God's safe hand;
Our hopes, ambitions, needs, and those we love,
Just see them, in his all-embracing care,
And say with joyous heart, "They are with Thee."

AUTHOR UNKNOWN

Faith

I want to write about faith,
   about the way the moon rises
      over cold snow, night after night,

faithful even as it fades from fullness,
   slowly becoming that last curving and impossible
      sliver of light before the final darkness.

But I have no faith myself
   I refuse it the smallest entry.

Let this then, my small poem,
   like a new moon, slender and barely open,
      be the first prayer that opens me to faith.

DAVID WHYTE

No Need to Worry

Good morning,
This is God!
I will be handling all your problems today.
I will not need your help—
so have a great day.

AUTHOR UNKNOWN

Who Builds a Church Within His Heart

Who builds a church within his heart
And takes it with him everywhere
Is holier far than he whose church
Is but a one-day house of prayer.

MORRIS ABEL BEER

Psalm 23 for Busy People

The Lord is my pace-setter, I shall not rush;
he makes me stop and rest for quiet intervals,
he provides me with images of stillness,
which restore my serenity.
He leads me in the way of efficiency,
through calmness of mind,
and his guidance is peace.
Even though I have a great many things
    to accomplish each day.
I will not fret, for his presence is here.
His timelessness, his all–importance
    will keep me in balance.

He prepares refreshment and renewal
in the midst of activity,
by anointing my mind with his oils of tranquility
my cup of joyous energy overflows.
Surely harmony and effectiveness shall be
the fruits of my hours
and I shall walk in the pace of my Lord,
and dwell in his house for ever.

TOKI MIYASHINA

The Lord Is My Shepherd

The Lord is my shepherd; I shall not want.

He maketh me to lie down in green pastures: he leadeth me beside still waters.

He restoreth my soul: he leadeth me in paths of righteousness for his name's sake.

Yea, though I walk through the valley of the shadow of death, I will fear no evil: for thou art with me; thy rod and thy staff they comfort me.

Thou preparest a table before me in the presence of mine enemies; thou anointest my head with oil; my cup runneth over.

Surely goodness and mercy shall follow me all the days of my life: and I will dwell in the house of the Lord forever.

PSALM 23

The Beatitudes

Blessed are the poor in spirit:
    for theirs is the kingdom of heaven.
Blessed are they that mourn:
    for they shall be comforted.
Blessed are the meek:
    for they shall inherit the earth.
Blessed are they which do hunger and thirst after
    righteousness:
    for they shall be filled.
Blessed are the merciful:
    for they shall obtain mercy.
Blessed are the pure in heart:
    for they shall see God.
Blessed are the peace-makers:
    for they shall be called the children of God.

MATTHEW 5:3–9

Faith

Heart of Gold

Help me to remember, Lord,
When suffering seems unfair,
You test our faith, You test our strength,
You test how much we care.

As the test of gold is fire,
Letting purity unfold,
You take our spirit, try to clear it,
And forge a heart of gold.

MARY PAT STRENGER LOOMIS

The Thing Is

The thing is
to love life
to love it even when you have no
stomach for it, when everything you've held
dear crumbles like burnt paper in your hands
and your throat is filled with the silt of it.
When grief sits with you so heavily
it is like heat, tropical, moist
thickening the air so it's heavy like water
more fit for gills than lungs.
When grief weights you like your own flesh
only more of it, an obesity of grief.
How long can a body withstand this, you think,
and yet you hold life like a face between your
     palms,
a plain face, with no charming smile
or twinkle in her eye,
and you say, yes, I will take you
I will love you, again.

ELLEN BASS

Faith

35

Wild Geese

When I hear a trumpet call
From autumn's evening sky,
I feel a quiet humility
As wild geese journey by.
It is of my mortality
I am reminded when
They signal something sacred
In another season's end.

I contemplate the message
These wild geese have implied,
That they have put their trust in one
Whose voice will be their guide,
And as I watch with reverence,
My own faith is renewed
By wild geese interrupting
My autumn solitude.

HILDA SANDERSON

I Believe

I believe in the sun even when it does not shine
I believe in love even when I do not feel it
I believe in God even when He is silent.

AUTHOR UNKNOWN

HOPE

Look to This Day

Look to this day,
For it is life,
The very life of life.
In its brief course lie all
The realities and verities of existence,
The bliss of growth,
The splendor of action,
The glory of power—

For yesterday is but a dream,
And tomorrow is only a vision,
But today, well lived,
Makes every yesterday a dream of happiness
And every tomorrow a vision of hope.

SANSKRIT PROVERB

Hope

The faintest of whispers: the softest of sighs,
a "did I see something" obliquely pass by?

a movement that speaks; a presence that loves,
a rustle of gossamer; myriad doves.

not much is required; so little we need,
the smallest of dreams, a mere mustard seed.

a glimpse, or a glimmer, a flicker of light,
a promise of day against vapid night.

hope.

SUZANNE GROSSER

It Took the Worst Day

It took the worst day
when there was
nothing left to do, when
even my tears were exhausted
and I was empty
as a parched jug, cracked dry.

That was when I walked outside,
stood by the lemon tree and
rubbed the dust off one leaf
with my thumb, held the
cool glossy surface to my cheek
and was surprised by its pungent smell.

ELLEN BASS

This, Too, Shall Pass

In times of trial an old Indian legend has given me much comfort. A king who suffered many hours of discouragement urged his courtiers to devise a motto, short enough to be engraved on a ring, which should be suitable alike in prosperity and in adversity. After many suggestions had been rejected, his daughter offered an emerald bearing the inscription in Arabic "This, too, shall pass."

Said the poet:

Whate'er thou art, where'er thy footsteps stray,
    Heed these wise words: This, too, shall pass
        away.
Oh, jewel sentence from the mine of truth!
    What riches it contains for age or youth.
No stately epic, measured and sublime,
    So comforts, or so counsels, for all time
As these few words. Go write them on your heart
    And make them of your daily life a part.
Art thou in misery, brother? Then I pray
    Be comforted! Thy grief shall pass away.
Art thou elated? Ah, be not too gay;

Temper thy joy, *this, too,* shall pass away.
Fame, glory, place and power,
    They are but little baubles of the hour.
Thus, be not o'er proud,
    Nor yet cast down; judge thou aright;
When skies are clear, expect the cloud;
    In darkness, wait the coming light;
Whatever be thy fate today,
    Remember, *even this*, shall pass away!

ADAPTED BY A. L. ALEXANDER
from sources including
Paul Hamilton Hayne, John Godfrey Saxe, and Ella Wheeler Wilcox

After the Long Gathering

After the long gathering
You will enter a silence
Of stones,
Of leaves,
Of wings.

You will hear
That when anything ends
A singing begins.

This singing has been
Part of you
Since the beginning of time.
It comes to break the tide,
To pierce the dark
And make you green again.

After the long gathering
You will enter a silence
Of stones,
Of leaves
Of wings.

CORRINE DE WINTER

On the Holy Breath of Wind

The seed, carried in hands, hearts,
or on the holy breath of wind,
drifts . . .
falls casually
in unrecognized perfection
to where the measure of the sun to shade,
of dry to wet,
of promise to past
or scar to hope,
seems hopeless.

Yet there underneath something grows,
outside the rows of the planned for.

God keep me mindful
of a mind beyond my own.
Lead me not into my own landscaping
but waken me please,
to the exquisite, elegant weed.

RENÉE MACKENZIE

Hope

The Good News

The good news
they do not print.
The good news
we do print.
We have a special edition every moment,
and we need you to read it.
The good news is that you are alive,
that the linden tree is still there,
standing firm in the harsh Winter.
The good news is that you have wonderful eyes
to touch the blue sky.
The good news is that your child is there before
        you,
and your arms are available:
hugging is possible.
They only print what is wrong.
Look at each of our special editions.
We always offer the things that are not wrong.
We want you to benefit from them
and help protect them.
The dandelion is there by the sidewalk,
smiling its wondrous smile,

singing the song of eternity.
Listen! You have ears that can hear it.
Bow your head.
Listen to it.
Leave behind the world of sorrow
and preoccupation
and get free.
The latest good news
is that you can do it.

THICH NHAT HANH

Coincidence

Coincidence is God's way
of remaining anonymous.

AUTHOR UNKNOWN

Opportunity

To each being God has given
Much opportunity,
To find the joy of living life
With hope and dignity.

And as we go along the way,
There comes a time to know
When the path no longer goes
The way we want to go.

Exalted mute ambitions,
Thwarted hopes that fail,
Should sometimes be discarded
For things that serve us well—

And if, indeed, we really look,
Each one will surely see
All the many worthwhile fruits
Of opportunity.

So do not feel vexation with
An old and tainted star,
But be prepared to see afresh
The dreams that really are.

HILDA SANDERSON

Hope Is the Thing with Feathers

Hope is the thing with feathers
That perches in the soul,
And sings the tune without the words,
And never stops at all,

And sweetest in the gale is heard;
And sore must be the storm
That could abash the little bird
That kept so many warm.

I've heard it in the chillest land,
And on the strangest sea;
Yet, never, in extremity,
It asked a crumb of me.

EMILY DICKINSON
(1830–1866)

Hope

Living in Hope

When I feel most alone,
Hope holds my hand.
When sadness buckles me,
Hope helps me stand.
When circumstances overwhelm me,
Hope restores my energy.
When chores numb and bore me,
Hope glorifies them.
When I fear self-revelation,
Hope gives me courage to be myself.

To live in hope is to believe
in light when it is dark,
in beauty when ugliness abounds,
in peace when conflict reigns,
in love when hatred marches.

May I never stop hoping.

SuzAnne C. Cole

Auguries

This ground's a dead sea—
frozen mud, debris churned up
by winter frost heaves,
tractable as cement.
I prod and poke with an auger,
drill in the seed;
nothing can grow:
a season of zeroes,
a garden of stones.

But I will keep faith:
on the day of St. Patrick,
I will plant peas,
praying for green.
I will believe in June,
the return of the sun,
and I will taste the snap
of sugar
on my hungering tongue.

BARBARA CROOKER

Oak Trees of Hope

O God, take our tiny acorns of service
and turn them into
towering oak trees of hope.

MARIAN WRIGHT EDELMAN

The Inner Flame

I am not more than
a wisp
   of
      smoke
to the world,
but
to God
I am a flame of hope and promise
in a darkened room.

JOAN NOËLDECHEN

COURAGE

Persistence

Lord, help me to keep moving ahead
when I want to give up and turn back.
Help me to put one foot in front of the other
to get over this new mountain
You've given to me to climb
on the way home to
You.

MARIAN WRIGHT EDELMAN

Give Us Courage

Give us courage, gaiety and the quiet mind.
Spare us to our friends, soften to us our enemies.
Bless us, if it may be, in all our innocent
    endeavors.
If it may not, give us the strength to encounter
that which is to come, that we be brave in peril,
constant in tribulation, temperate in wrath,
and in all changes of fortune and down to the
    gates
of death, loyal and loving one to another.

ROBERT LOUIS STEVENSON
(1850–1894)

Courage

The Main Thing

The entire world is a narrow bridge
But the main thing is not to fear.

<small>LIKUTEY MOHARAN 2:28</small>

There Will Come

into the dark of night
starshine

into the turmoil of day
an extra measure
of strength

into the hurricane
the eye of calm

into the inner heart
faith

but none of these
are seen
from behind shuttered
windows.

ELIZABETH SEARLE LAMB

Courage

62

For the Tree Outside My Window

We are not so different, after all;
the same force flows through both of us.
When I touch you, the pulse of your energy
makes my hand tingle.
We are part of the same whole;
you speak to me as clearly as if you had words.
Make roots, you say, plant yourself firmly
in soil which nurtures and strengthens
against drought or lack of sun.
Seek only to keep growing.
Accept gratefully whatever the earth gives.
If you live with its rhythms,
you will learn to bend.
There are marks on you,
evidence of brokenness and age;
do not think of them as scars:
they make you more beautiful.

BONITA FOGG SMITH

Courage

63

Endurance

The gem
cannot be polished
without friction,
nor man perfected
without trials.

Confucius
(551–479 b.c.)

Splendor in the Grass

Though nothing can bring back
the hour of splendor in the grass,
of glory in the flower;
we will grieve not,
rather find strength
in what remains behind.

WILLIAM WORDSWORTH
(1770-1850)

What Can't Be Cured

What can't be cured
must be endured.

FRANÇOIS RABELAIS
(1483–1553)

Run with the Moon

Run with the moon,
embrace the darkness,
grow hard with the cold,
put pain from your mind,
and on the last day,
you, alone, will
be friendly with the dark.

When you come
to face the thing you fear,
trust the Creator.

AUTHOR UNKNOWN

Never Be Defeated

See every difficulty
   as a challenge,
         a stepping stone,
and never be defeated
   by anything
         or anyone.

Eileen Caddy

Our Real Journey

It may be that when we no longer
    know what to do,
we have come to our real work,
    and when we no longer
know which way to go,
    we have begun our real journey.

WENDELL BERRY

HEALING

Restoration

I breathe,
Slowly through my nostrils
Capturing particles
of air
That travel to my lungs, in harmony
With Life
Surrounding me.

I release an essence
With every parting breath,
Trees, flowers, weeds
Synthesize the gas
And exhale the oxygen
Through structures
As delicate as butterfly wings.
In our interdependence
We sanctify each other with Life
Each breath a blessing
A restoration, an act of healing.

SHIRLEY KOBAR

Hot Tea Therapy

All of us
need Hot Tea Therapy
        from time to time,
Requiring a special someone
who lets us know
        by word
                and
                        deed
that another cares,
Whether it's to mend a broken dream,
Repair a damaged expectation,
Celebrate the smallest success,
Give a single hug of encouragement
Or simply share a cup of hot tea.

SUSAN NORTON

Woman to Woman

I am no stranger.
I am a woman like you
mending after illness.
I would take the fear
palpable as a walnut
out of your body,
the fear that something
can erase our breath.
Somewhere inside
a wisdom larger than us
knows the course of our lives
and carries the weight
of our pain and fear,
and offers with tender hands
the faith and understanding
that leads to healing.

MARIAN OLSON

Healing

Healing Hands

Dear God, let my hands
be always hands of healing
through which your Life
may radiate to lessen pain,
to bring a renewal of peace
and healing wherever needed.

Dear God, let my hands
bring through their touch
some essence of Your love
flowing through them
to bring comfort and joy.
I offer my hands as a channel;
use them as Your healing tools.

ELIZABETH SEARLE LAMB

When I'm Weary

When I'm weary,
And no longer
Hear Your voice,
I take it up
The mountain
To breathe
Your Blessing
Where pines
Are as tall
As cathedrals,
And silence
Is broken
By footfalls
As I walk
Your aisles
Of well-trodden paths.

SHIRLEY KOBAR

A Healing Prayer

In silence now
I open my mind,
my heart and spirit
to God, who is ever
the One Healer.

O God, let love
erase imperfection.
Let peace soothe
every nerve.
Let joy re-energize
my whole body.

In silence now
I let go and let
the total perfection
that *is* God be
the total truth
of my whole being
at this very moment
and for always.

ELIZABETH SEARLE LAMB

For One in Grief

We know you're feeling sorrow
And sense your grief is deep;
But you have a thousand memories
That you will always keep.

To live in hearts still beating—
Is not to die in vain—
For love and thought are endless
and forever will remain.

JOAN STEPHEN

Time

They say that "time assuages,"—
Time never did assuage;
An actual suffering strengthens,
As sinews do, with age.

Time is a test of trouble,
But not a remedy.
If such is prove, it prove too
There was no malady.

EMILY DICKINSON
(1830-1886)

Joy

You speak to me
in the silence,
Your voice the chinook.
You heal me
in the beauty
of the pine forests.
I am filled
with Your presence
in the gentle fall
of snow on a mountain trail.
Blessed, by the incense of Your flowers.
Joy is mine
to see the eagle in flight
feathers curled upward
catching thermals.
Your beneficence
is everywhere, if only
I have the eyes
to see.

SHIRLEY KOBAR

COMPASSION

Gentle Me, Lord

Gentle me, Lord, so I can see past self-interest.
So I am not judgmental but compassionate.
So I am not selfish but helpful to others.
So I laugh at myself and with others.
So I am tolerant and patient.
So I am grateful for life.
Gentle me, Lord, so I see with my heart.

PHYLLIS JOY DAVISON

Beatitudes for Disabled People

Blessed are you who take time
to listen to defective speech,
for you help us to know that
if we persevere, we can be
understood.

Blessed are you who walk with
us in public places and ignore
the stares of strangers, for in
your companionship we find
havens of relaxation.

Blessed are you that never bids
us "hurry up" and more blessed
are you that do not snatch our tasks
from our hands to do them for us,
for often we need time rather than help.

Blessed are you who stand beside
us as we enter new ventures, for
our failures will be outweighed
by times we surprise
ourselves and you.

Blessed are you who ask for
our help, for our greatest need
is to be needed.

Blessed are you when by all these
things you assure us that the
thing that makes us individuals
is not our peculiar muscles,
nor our wounded nervous system,
but is the God-given self
that no infirmity can
confine.

MARJORIE CHAPPELL

My Religion

My religion is very simple—
my religion is kindness.

THE DALAI LAMA

Compassion

No One Walks Alone

That no one's heart is empty,
That no one goes unfed,
That no one harms another,
That no one feels he has no brother,
That each and every one of us,
Lets the light within us shine,
That no one walks
Through darkness alone.

AUTHOR UNKNOWN

A Wish

But what a different country
this would be if angry blaming voices
mellowed into a chorus that understood:
"There but for the grace of God go I."

ELLEN GOODMAN

FORGIVENESS

Teach Us to Forgive

(Forgiveness)

Lord, teach us to forgive:
to look deep into the hearts
of those who wound us,
so that we may glimpse,
in that dark, still water,
not just the reflection
of our own face
but yours as well.

SHEILA CASSIDY

Father Forgive

This poem was written after the bombing of the Coventry cathedral in England, on November 22, 1943, by the Germans. It is placed in the bombed-out remains of the Emperor Wilhelm Memorial Church, in Berlin, Germany. A cross of nails, from the remains of the Coventry cathedral, was represented in a ceremony on January 7, 1987, as an act of reconciliation. There are now such crosses of nails in Dresden, in what used to be East Berlin, and in Volgograd (formerly Stalingrad) in Russia.

The hatred which separates race from race,
nation from nation, class from class—
      Father forgive.
The covetous striving of person and peoples
to possess what is not their own—
      Father forgive.
The greed for possessions which exploits
the labor of people and destroys the earth—
      Father forgive.
Our envy of the prosperity of others—
      Father forgive.

Our lack of sympathy for the distress of
the homeless and refugees—
        Father forgive.
Our desire to misuse the bodies of men and
    women
for immoral purposes—
        Father forgive.
Our pride, which misleads us to place confidence
in ourselves, and not in God—
        Father forgive.

AUTHOR UNKNOWN

In Forgetting There Is Forgiveness

There is no forgiveness
save in reaching beyond;
there is no letting go
save in moving on—
in movement there is healing,
in healing there is forgetting,
in forgetting there is forgiveness.

RABBI RAMI M. SHAPIRO

Openhearted Sharing

When feelings are hurt, Wise Physician, we curl in upon ourselves like orange rinds, withholding even the possibility of reconciliation and peace. Let us be open to the honest sharing of others without becoming resentful and close-hearted. Help us awaken to new possibilities for righting wrongs, forgiving, and loving without reservation as the orange blossom offers its fragrance, the fruit its zesty sweetness.

MARGARET ANNE HUFFMAN

What Forgiveness

Austere is that Forgiveness
which rules from awesome throne
and designates conditions
before it can begin.

Far better is Forgiveness
which walks along with purpose,
forgetful of each misstep
and even a fall from grace.

MARYANNE HANNAN

And Then

And then a vast, surprising peacefulness
descended, like a blue shadow upon
the snow; and the shadow sleeping on the snow
was a kind of reconciliation, form
embraced by content, light by light, the birds
hanging from the branches like bright red berries.

And then for days, there was nothing to disturb
the beauty of that equilibrium,
which was so like the miracle of forgiveness.

KELLY CHERRY

PEACE

Peace in Our Homes

May it prevail in this household . . .
May our words be gentle, our actions loving,
Our intentions honorable . . .
For a peaceful world can be created only by those
who practice peace, each moment of each day
in their hearts and in their homes.

CAROLINE JOY ADAMS

Peace Is Looming

Great Grandmother Spirit,
teach us to weave ten million thoughts
and sing them in our minds,
that war may loom no more.

Great Great Grandmother,
teach us to weave ten hundred words
and write them in our hearts,
that we sow war no more.

Great Great Great Grandmother,
make us weave deeds ten thousand strong,
and dance them holding hands.
No more wars.

Spin your necklace of stars around our necks,
so we speak in constellations
of friendship, hope, forgiveness.
We'll hum the song from your loom of peace
against the dark.

WAVE CARBERRY

Pray for Your Enemies

Pray for your enemies, that they may be holy
and that all may be well with them.
And should you think this is not serving God,
rest assured that more than all prayers,
this is indeed the service of God.

THE TALMUD

Peace Begins

When we open our hearts
Calm rushes in—
Kindness flows out;
Peace then begins.
Love overpowers—
Intolerance ends;
There is no more hating
And caring begins.

JOAN STEPHEN

The Serenity Prayer

God grant me the serenity
to accept the things I cannot change,
the courage to change the things I can,
and the wisdom to know the difference.

REINHOLD NIEBUHR
(1892–1971)

Letting Go

When the day
has been lived
I let it go;
when a cycle
is done, I
release it.
I let the past
be no more
than an echo
in this present day,
knowing myself
free to move
toward new joy
and grow toward
a closer oneness
with God.

ELIZABETH SEARLE LAMB

Peace

At Peace Am I

Flowers every night
Blossom in the sky;
Peace in the Infinite,
At peace am I.

RUMI
(1207–1273)

APPRECIATION

It Would Be a Blessing

I have often thought it would be a blessing
if each human being were stricken blind and deaf
for a few days during early adult life.
Darkness would make one more appreciative of
sight
and silence would teach one the joys of sound.

HELEN KELLER
(1880–1968)

A Place Remembered

In the shadows of our mind
Lives a place of long ago
That time will never change
Because we loved it so.

A country lane less travel worn,
The house all trimmed in white,
Twilight song of peepers
On a tranquil summer's night.

The flowers bloomed eternal
With a sky of endless blue;
It was a piece of heaven
Where all our dreams came true.

Visions of our loved ones,
They live and always will—
For no one ever dies in
The place that time stands still.

It was a special sanctum
From where we left to roam;
A hideaway of yesterday—
Our hearts still call it home.

C. DAVID HAY

Precious Moments

Rainbows and roses after the rain,
The splendor of twilight embracing the plain ...
Strolls by the seaside beneath a full moon,
A butterfly's flight from an empty cocoon.
A carpet of leaves of pure autumn gold,
Reflections of love in the young and the old ...
Blossoms of apple and cherry and plum,
The joy of a child when Christmas has come.
The beauty of sunset setting the hillside aglow,
The wonder and peace of new fallen snow ...
Bees making honey, the glory of spring,
A mockingbird learning a new song to sing.
The stillness of dawn's pale lavender skies,
The leaping of hearts when a baby first cries ...
The splendor and grace of an eagle in flight,
The silence of stars guarding the night.
A baby's first step, a daughter's first prayer,
Our flag proudly waving in cool mountain air ...
A lover's first kiss, a hug from a friend,
It's these precious moments we pray never end.

CLAY HARRISON

i thank You God for most this amazing

i thank You God for most this amazing
day: for the leaping greenly spirits of trees
and a blue true dream of sky; and for everything
which is natural which is infinite which is yes

E. E. CUMMINGS
(1894–1962)

Appreciation

116

Confiteor

I confess today I got lost in technicalities.
Like folding an origami crane I paid so much
attention to folding, bending and creasing
the right way, I didn't notice I was creating
a colorful creature with wings to fly and soar.
Tomorrow let me be aware of the miracles that
      unfold.

SUSAN J. ERICKSON

Saying Grace

Start with one
cup rice, two cups
water. Do not stir
while rice boils.
Do not talk.
                Breathe.

Pour oil, soy sauce
into cast iron skillet.
Grate ginger, chop
carrots, dice green
onions and broccoli.
                Rest.

Combine with rice.
Scoop into wide
mouth bowl.
Fill tall glass
Appreciation   with cool water.
118   Sit.

Notice the light.
Imagine everything
you love is in
front of you. Take
small mouthfuls.
                    Pray.

STEPHEN J. LYONS

Neighbors

Neighbors who don't interfere
Neighbors who listen
Neighbors with a willing arm
    to harvest a field or can abundant fruit
    or bring in chicken soup
    when the body aches with illness
Neighbors who laugh and play
    and neighbors who can cry with you or be
    a sounding board
        for silly jokes or questions about existence:
        God, pain, love
Neighbors who can leave each other alone
    when it's time to be alone
Neighbors who are friends

MARIAN OLSON

Appreciation

120

Every Day

Every day is a god
each day is a god,
and holiness holds forth in time.
I worship each god,
I praise each day splintered down,
splintered down and wrapped in time like a husk,
a husk of many colors spreading, at dawn
fast over the mountains split.

ANNIE DILLARD

Tulip

I watched its first green push
through bare dirt, where the builders
had dropped boards, shingles, plaster—
killing everything.
I could not recall what grew there,
what returned each spring,
but the leaves looked tulip,
and one morning it arrived,
a scarlet slash against the aluminum siding.

Mornings, on the way to my car,
I bow to the still bell
of its closed petals; evenings
it greets me, light ringing
at the end of my driveway.

Sometimes I kneel
to stare into the yellow throat,
count the black tongues,
stroke the firm red mouth.
It opens and closes my days.
It has made me weak with love,
this god I didn't know I needed.

PENNY HARTER

Eternity

To see a World in a Grain of Sand
And a Heaven in a Wild Flower,
Hold Infinity in the palm of your hand
And Eternity in an hour.

WILLIAM BLAKE
(1757–1827)

GRATITUDE

Kneeling to Pick Flowers

There is a God
in whose name I praise
trees, rivers, stars,

quiet hours
in woods and orchards,
I pray when I kneel
to pick flowers.

JENNIFER STANLEY

For What We Have Today

I heard my little boy one day
Kneel down and fold his hands to pray;
The words he spoke were all his own,
No formal prayer as yet he'd known.

I watched him as he raised his head
And looked at Heaven; then he said:
"God, take care of what we have today!"
That's all there was for him to say.

He rose and tumbled into bed
Serene and sure in what he said.

And oh, how deep the thought struck me,
How foolish we must seem to be
To our Creator when WE pray
To give us this or that today.

Perhaps a thank-you now and then
Just to show courtesy again;
But greater wisdom, purer joy
Came from lips of my small boy!
Now in MY prayers I always say:
"God, please take care of what we have TODAY!"

LILLIAN J. LOYD

The Best Is Now and Here

No longer forward or behind
I look in hope or fear
But grateful take the good I find
the best is now and here.

JOHN GREENLEAF WHITTIER
(1807–1892)

The Present

The past is history,
the future is a mystery,
and this moment is a gift.
That is why this moment
is called *the present*.

<small>AUTHOR UNKNOWN</small>

Gratitude

I Love You, Gentlest of Ways

I love you, gentlest of Ways,
who ripened us as we wrestled with you.

You, the great homesickness we could never shake
    off,
you, the forest that always surrounded us,

you, the song we sang in every silence,
your dark net threading through us,

on the day you made us you created yourself,
and we grew sturdy in your sunlight....

Let your hand rest on the rim of Heaven now
and mutely bear the darkness we bring over you.

RAINER MARIA RILKE
(1875–1926)
(Translated by Anita Barrows and Joanna Macy)

Give Us This Day

Today you've given me sunshine, Lord
with washing winds to cleanse the air,
the many-voiced mocking bird
sings songs he needs to share.

A brave, determined ant
carried a crumb
twice his size,
hurrying past my patient feet
to colonize his prize.

A black and orange monarch
flutters—
teasingly,
above a quenching brook:
Lord, you've given me another day—
To be
To breathe
To look.

JILL MORGAN HAWKINS

Silence

Sometimes we forget the blessing of silence.
Sometimes the wind is poem enough,
the way a mountain hunches, the play
of the sun across ocean in the space of a day.
Sometimes moss is a stanza, the orange of lichen
will stand in for a sonnet on a day like that.

RICHARD BEBAN

Take Nothing for Granted

Take nothing for granted: the sheer act
of waking each day; fresh air upon your cheek;
each effort expended on self or another—
walking the dog, shopping for food, toiling
at home   in an office   or on the road.
Every moment is rare, short and full of glory.
Every word is magic, a story achieved through
        will.
Marvel at nature's moods as mirror of your own.
Recall a sunrise or sunset, a flock of geese in the
        sky.
Care about parents or children as fragile gifts
like petal on a rose, like song from one bird.
Praise the simple or complex—the invention of
        flight
above clouds; the wheel; the bathtub; a rocking-
        chair.
We rise and fall in the moon or a wave,
in a smile or many tears. And being brave
is to be alive as we give and share love
always, only and ever to survive.

ROCHELLE LYNN HOLT

JOY

All

Even sitting
at the kitchen table
in the frizzy heat
of an August afternoon
is a cosmic experience.
The sweet garden carrot
crunching in my mouth
becomes me.
All is spirit.

KATE ROBINSON

God's World

O World, I cannot hold thee close enough!
   Thy winds, thy wide grey skies!
   Thy mists, that roll and rise!
Thy woods, this autumn day, that ache and sag
And all but cry with colour! That gaunt crag
To crush! To lift the lean of the black bluff!
World, World, I cannot get thee close enough!

EDNA ST. VINCENT MILLAY
(1892–1950)

Simple Joy

May the simple joy of:

a sprightly red radish on crusty bread,
a crescent moon slicing the dusky sky,
laundry warm from the dryer,
the spicy perfume of an orange being peeled,
rain tiptoeing on the roof at night,

be yours and mine

SUSAN J. ERICKSON

The Cup of Life

Take this cup,
I've filled it up,
with love and joy and laughter.
Now it's empty,
Fill it up.
Repeat,
Forever after.
First, so full
I'm giving
All my love and joy in living.
Then near empty,
Tired of living,
And I'm the
One who needs the giving.
This cup, this cup,
this cup of life,
It's always overflowing;
We give and get
And get and give,
Life's balance
Keeps on going.
Take this cup,

I've filled it up,
With love and joy and laughter.
Now it's empty,
Fill it up.
Repeat,
Forever, after.

LAURA BYRNES

Traditional Hindu Wisdom

One of the best ways to worship God
is simply to be happy.

AUTHOR UNKNOWN

WONDER

Epiphany

It was Einstein who said
either nothing is a miracle,
or everything is—
a jagged mountain range,
lilacs in bloom,
a peacock unfurled,
sun on your arm,
the touch of a stranger.

Take your pick: be surprised
by nothing at all,
or by everything that is.

MARYANNE HANNAN

How Did You Think of a Star?
(God the Artist)

God, when you thought of a pine tree,
    How did you think of a star?
God, when you patterned a bird song,
    Flung on a silver string,
How did you know the ecstasy
    That crystal call would bring?
How did you think of a bubbling throat
    And a beautifully speckled wing?

God, when you fashioned a raindrop,
    How did you think of a stem
Bearing a lovely satin leaf
    To hold the tiny gem?
How did you know a million drops
    Would deck the morning's hem?

Why did you mate the moonlit night
    With the honeysuckle vines?
How did you know Madeira bloom
    Distilled ecstatic wines?

How did you weave the velvet dusk
    Where tangled perfumes are?
God, when you thought of a pine tree,
    How did you think of a star?

ANGELA MORGAN

Miracles

Why, who makes much of a miracle?
As to me I know of nothing else but miracles,
Whether I walk the streets of Manhattan . . .
Or look at strangers opposite me riding in the car,
Or watch honey-bees busy around the hive of a
     summer forenoon,
Or animals feeding in the fields,
Or birds, or the wonderfulness of insects in the air,
Or the wonderfulness of the sundown, or of stars
     shining so quiet and bright,
Or the exquisite delicate thin curve of the new
     moon in spring . . .
To me every hour of the light and dark is a
     miracle,
Every cubic inch of space is a miracle,
Every square yard of the surface of the earth is
     spread with the same,
Every foot of the interior swarms with the same. . . .
What stranger miracles are there?

WALT WHITMAN
(1819–1892)

From Within

How sublime—
a boat beneath the moon
and from within, a prayer.

KOZAN, EIGHTEENTH-CENTURY JAPANESE POET

When I Heard the Learn'd Astronomer

When I heard the learn'd astronomer,
When the proofs, the figures, were ranged in
    columns before me,
When I was shown the charts and diagrams,
    to add, divide, and measure them,
When I sitting heard the astronomer where he
    lectured with much applause in the lecture-
       room,
How soon unaccountable I became tired and sick,
Till rising and gliding out I wander'd off by
    myself,
In the mystical moist night-air, and from time to
    time
Look'd up in perfect silence at the stars.

WALT WHITMAN
(1819–1892)

Magic

We were talking about magic
as we drove along a crowded
Sunday highway

when the whir of wings
made me turn
and a flock of geese

flew over our car
so low I could see
their feet tucked under them.

For a moment the rustle
of their presence over our heads
obscured everything

and as they disappeared
you said,
"I see what you mean."

JENIFER NOSTRAND

Deer at the Door

What drew them up the hill, away
from sheltering pines, overgrown sumac,
    everything
in leaf now that summer's nearly here?
Was it light inside this little house,
our soft conversation, our attention
to the roast, the salad, before us?
What is it they saw, standing by the window,
their gentle heads raised, then browsing
again in the grass? Was it our shadows
bent over our plates, our acceptance
of what we have, what we are,
as the slow weight of day began to leave?
—I remember the beginning of a moment:
the sparrow's throat opening, the dog
rising from her place on the rug, me standing, you
looking up, the song starting, the dog and I
crossing the room, my hand on the door,
the smiles on our faces, the song on its last notes,
everything in harmony for a few beats of the
    heart.
Then the door opened

and their heads lifted, the air turned still.
I heard the rustle of grass, saw their white tails
　　flash
as they darted awkwardly down the hill,
and dusk came on like the closing of an eye.

JUDITH MINTY

God

I greet you in the softness of unexpected snow
As the ground wakes from winter slumber
In the white coats of dogwood at river's edge
Pressed by spring rain

As laughter sounds between lovers at dusk
When the east wind dances with the bare tree
During summer's resplendent parade

My heart rejoices
At our meetings

Lora Robertson

The Angel of Garage Sales

guides us, when we find a hand-glazed brown
and blue coffee mug among chipped china,
milk glass vases, plastic flowers. She hovers
nearby, when a white porcelain teapot
in the shape of a hen, delicately
painted with cornflower blue, calls from a pile
of avocado and harvest gold bowls.
She points out the rhinestone-studded apron,
the wooden carving of a crocodile, the crocheted
vest. Did you feel her tap your shoulder
when you found the sweater knit in a pattern
of webs and spiders the year your son discovered
insects? Did you feel the brush of her wings?
Was it the glint of her halo or just the silvery
rain on the street as she passed by?

BARBARA CROOKER

Sylvan

The quietude of the forest,
like a grand cathedral,
welcomes me.
Every leaf is divinity,
every tree holds
a moment of eternity.

CORRINE DE WINTER

CONTEMPLATION

Live the Question

…have patience with everything that remains
unsolved in your heart. Try to love the *questions
themselves*, like locked rooms and like books
written in a foreign language. Do not now look
for the answers. They cannot now be given to you
because you could not live them. It is a question
of experiencing everything. At present you need
to *live* the question. Perhaps you will gradually,
without even noticing it, find yourself
experiencing the answer, some distant day.

RAINER MARIA RILKE
(1875–1926)

A Servant's Words

My life is not my own.

I cannot take a breath,
build a dream,
bury a seed,
or open a window
unless God permits it.

Somehow,
God is carving my soul
with the chisel of time
and through each stroke . . .

I keep surrendering,
and surrendering,
and surrendering.

MIKE W. BLOTTENBERGER

Contemplation

160

Some Keep the Sabbath Going to Church

Some keep the Sabbath going to Church—
I keep it, staying at Home—
With a Bobolink for a Chorister—
And an Orchard, for a Dome—

Some keep the Sabbath in Surplice—
I just wear my Wings—
And instead of tolling the Bell, for Church,
Our little Sexton—sings.

God preaches, a noted Clergyman—
And sermon is never long,
So instead of getting to Heaven, at last—
I'm going, all along.

EMILY DICKINSON
(1830-1886)

Better Trust All

Better trust all and be deceived,
  And weep that trust and that deceiving,
Than doubt one heart that, if believed,
  Had blessed one's life with true believing.

FANNY KEMBLE
(1809–1893)

Grace

It becomes easier
to be considerate,
to be kind
when you realize
every face encountered
contains the grace of God.
It is easy to find purpose,
to see the meaning
in simple things
when you're aware that each
action, every effort
brings you closer
to the gentle hand
of God.

CORRINE DE WINTER

Those We Love the Best

One great truth in life I've found,
    While journeying to the West—
The only folks we really wound
    Are those we love the best.

The man you thoroughly despise
    Can rouse your wrath, 'tis true;
Annoyance in your heart will rise
    At things mere strangers do.

But those are only passing ills;
    This rule all lives will prove;
The rankling wound which aches and thrills
    Is dealt by hands we love.

The choicest garb, the sweetest grace,
    Are oft to strangers shown;
The careless mien, the frowning face,
    Are given to our own.

We flatter those we scarcely know,
    We please the fleeting guest,
And deal full many a thoughtless blow
    To those we love the best. . . .

ELLA WHEELER WILCOX
(1850–1919)

The World We Make

We make the world in which we live
By what we gather and what we give,
By our daily deeds and the things we say,
By what we keep or we cast away.

We make our world by the beauty we see
In a skylark's song or a lilac tree,
In a butterfly's wing, in the pale moon's rise,
And the wonder that lingers in midnight skies.

We make our world by the life we lead,
By the friends we have, by the books we read,
By the pity we show in the hour of care,
By the loads we lift and the love we share.

We make our world by the goals we pursue,
By the heights we seek and the higher view,
By hopes and dreams that reach the sun
And a will to fight till the heights are won.

Contemplation

165

What is the place in which we dwell,
A hut or a palace, a heaven or hell,
We gather and scatter, we take and we give,
We make our world—and there we live.

ALFRED GRANT WALTON

In the Middle

of a life that's as complicated as everyone else's,
struggling for balance, juggling time.
The mantel clock that was my grandfather's
has stopped at 9:20; we haven't had time
to get it repaired. The brass pendulum is still,
the chimes don't ring. One day you look out
the window, green summer, the next, and the leaves
have already fallen, and a grey sky lowers the horizon.
Our children almost grown, our parents gone,
it happened so fast. Each day, we must learn again
how to love, between morning's quick coffee
and evening's slow return. Steam from a pot of soup
rises, mixing with the yeasty smell of baking bread.
Our bodies twine, and the big black dog pushes
his great head between; his tail is a metronome,
¾ time. We'll never get there,
Time is always ahead of us, running down the beach,
urging us on faster, faster, but sometimes

we take off our watches, sometimes we lie
in the hammock, caught between the mesh
of rope and the net of stars, suspended, tangled up
in love, running out of time.

BARBARA CROOKER

The Voice of God

I sought to hear the voice of God,
 And climbed the topmost steeple.
But God declared: "Go down again,
 I dwell among the people."

Louis I. Newman
(1893–1972)

Our Birth Is But a Sleep

Our birth is but a sleep and a forgetting:
The Soul that rises with us, our life's Star,
     Hath had elsewhere its setting,
       And cometh from afar:
     Not in entire forgetfulness,
     And not in utter nakedness,
But trailing clouds of glory do we come
     From God, who is our home:
Heaven lies about us in our infancy!

WILLIAM WORDSWORTH
(1770–1850)

Angels in Disguise

Be not forgetful
to entertain strangers:
for thereby
some have entertained angels
                unawares.

HEBREWS 13:2

Contemplation

Living in the Present

We should be blessed
if we lived in the present always,
and took advantage of every accident
   that befell us,
like the grass which confesses the influence
   of the slightest dew that falls on it;
and did not spend our time in atoning for the
   neglect of past opportunities. . . .
We loiter in winter
while it is already spring.

HENRY DAVID THOREAU
(1817–1862)

INSPIRATION

Up

I can see how it might be possible
for a man to look down upon the earth
and be an atheist, but I cannot conceive
how he could look up into the heavens
and say there is no God.

ABRAHAM LINCOLN

Life

Life can only
be understood
backwards; but it
must be lived forwards.

SOREN KIERKEGAARD
(1813–1859)

Go Forth

Go forth in every direction—
        for the happiness, the harmony,
    the welfare of the many.
Offer your heart, the seeds of
        your own understanding
    like a lamp overturned
  and re-lit again
        illuminating the darkness.

THE BUDDHA
(563–483 B.C.)

Prelude

For the world will not applaud, though its prizes,
   glittery honors, dazzling futures, dangle
   like fat blue plums on faraway trees.
For every river you slog through, every rocky hill
   you climb,
what is attainable turns to dust in
   your hands, ashes in your mouth,
and the world
   merely shrugs its beefy shoulders, turns
the spotlight
   on the next moth dancing in its flame.
Instead, think
   of spring, daffodils and narcissus, tulips, azaleas,
that flower gorgeously for a few days, without
   any reason,
the April sky that draws over us its tender
   blue blanket,
the new grass green with infinite hope.
Consider, then, trees that burst into blossom:
   redbuds, dogwoods,
magnolias, such exuberant bloom, a carpet
   of petals strewn

on the sidewalks where you walked
    to class.
For the cold truth is, life on earth is hard,
    love rocky and thorny
and thistled, but spring is renewable,
    an eternal library book,
from the first shy glimpse of snowdrops,
    to the green and gold days
of forsythia
    sprawled on the lawn, to this grand finale of iris,
        peony,
    poppy, this great commencement, this walk in
        the sun.
So may your roots find water, good earth, work to
    do. May you
blossom, lavish and profuse. Never forget
    that the heart is
a flower.
    Go and dance your hour on the lawn.

Inspiration

Dreams

Hold fast to dreams
For if dreams die
Life is a broken-winged bird
That cannot fly.

Hold fast to dreams
For when dreams go
Life is a barren field
Frozen with snow.

LANGSTON HUGHES
(1902–1967)

Today, Tonight and Tomorrow

Bless to me, O God, the earth beneath my feet,
Bless to me, O God, the path whereon I go,
Bless to me, O God, the people whom I meet,
Today, tonight and tomorrow.

CELTIC BLESSING

You Never Can Tell

You never can tell when you send a word
   Like an arrow shot from a bow
By an archer blind, be it cruel or kind,
   Just where it may chance to go.
It may pierce the breast of your dearest friend,
   Tipped with its poison or balm,
To a stranger's heart in life's great mart
   It may carry its pain or its calm.

You never can tell when you do an act
   Just what the result will be,
But with every deed you are sowing a seed,
   Though the harvest you may not see.
Each kindly act is an acorn dropped
   In God's productive soil;
You may not know, but the tree shall grow
   With shelter for those who toil.

You never can tell what your thoughts will do
   In bringing you hate or love,
For thoughts are things, and their airy wings
   Are swifter than carrier doves.
They follow the law of the universe—

Each thing must create its kind,
And they speed o'er the track to bring you back
   Whatever went out from your mind.

ELLA WHEELER WILCOX
(1850–1919)

Star Wish

I saw a shooting star
As it blazed across the night
And marveled at the beauty
Of such a fleeting sight.

For one brief fiery instant
It flamed for all to see,
Then faded into darkness—
A brilliant memory.

Countless lights in endless space,
The splendor of the skies—
A star is always brightest
Just before it dies.

God grant me such a blessing
That peers may someday say—
I had my shining moment
As I passed this way.

Inspiration

184

C. DAVID HAY

Life's Mirror

There are loyal hearts, there are spirits brave,
   There are souls that are pure and true;
Then give to the world the best you have,
   And the best will come back to you.

Give love, and love to your life will flow,
   A strength in your utmost need;
Have faith, and a score of hearts will show
   Their faith in your word and deed.

Give truth, and your gift will be paid in kind,
   And honor will honor meet;
And a smile that is sweet will surely find
   A smile that is just as sweet.

Give sorrow and pity to those who mourn;
   You will gather in flowers again
The scattered seeds of your thought outborne
   Though the sowing seemed but vain.

For life is the mirror of king and slave—
   'Tis just what we are and do;
Then give to the world the best you have,
   And the best will come back to you.

Inspiration

185

"MADELINE BRIDGES"
(Mary Ainge de Vere)

The Most Vital Thing in Life

When you feel like saying something
  That you know you will regret,
Or keenly feel an insult
  Not quite easy to forget,
That's the time to curb resentment
  And maintain a mental peace,
For when your mind is tranquil
  All your ill-thoughts simply cease.

It is easy to be angry
  When defrauded or defied,
To be peeved and disappointed
  If your wishes were denied;
But to win a worthwhile battle
  Over selfishness and spite,
You must learn to keep strict silence
  Though you know you're in the right.

So keep your mental balance
  When confronted by a foe,
Be it enemy in ambush,
  Or some danger that you know.

If you are poised and tranquil
   When all around is strife,
Be assured that you have mastered
   The most vital thing in life.

GRENVILLE KLEISER
(1868–1953)

The Gardener's Toast

May your garden have lilies;
your window a view.
May your barn have an owl
and your lovers be true.

May your fences be friendly,
have gates, no barbed-wire.
May your smoke-house stand tall
and never catch fire.

May your apple trees bear
luscious fruit without scab,
and your pots in the sea
fill with Dungeness crab.

May your dogs never chase
after black cows or cars,
and your nights never be
without candles or stars.

May you always have one or two
bucks in your pockets,
and friends, on the Fourth,
who like picnics and rockets.

May the watercress grow
lush and green in your creek.
May your well overflow,
and your roof never leak.

THELMA PALMER

Harmony

May all I say and all I think
be in harmony with thee,
God within me, God beyond me,
maker of the trees.

<small>CHINOOK PSALTER</small>

In All Endeavors

In all endeavors
Strive to celebrate
The spirit of the warrior . . .
Calm,
Centered,
Certain . . .
Whether tending to the flower garden
Or searching for the heart of the divine.

JO-ANNE ROWLEY

The Road

Here is the road: the light
comes and goes then returns again.
Be gentle with your fellow travelers
as they move through the world of stone and stars
whirling with you yet every one alone.
The road waits.
Do not ask questions but when it invites you
to dance at daybreak, say yes.
Each step is the journey; a single note the song.

ARLENE GAY LEVINE

SUBJECT INDEX

Author Index

Author Index

196

PERMISSIONS AND
ACKNOWLEDGMENTS

Grateful acknowledgment is made to the authors and publishers for the use of the following material. Every effort has been made to contact original sources. If notified, the publishers will be pleased to rectify an omission in future editions.

Bantam Doubleday Dell Publishing Group, Inc., for "This, Too, Shall Pass Away" by A. L. Alexander; "Who Builds A Church" by Morris Abel Beer; "Life's Mirror" by Madeline Bridges; "The Most Vital Thing in Life" by Greenville Kleiser; "How Did You Think of a Star?" (originally titled "God the Artist"); "The Voice of God" by Louis I. Newman; "Song" by Harold Sandoll; "The World We Make" by Alfred Grant Walton; "Love Much," "Those We Love the Best," and "You Never Can Tell" by Ella Wilcox Wheeler from *Poems That Touch the Heart,* compiled by A. L. Alexander. Copyright © 1941 by Bantam Doubleday Dell; "The Human Touch" by Spencer Michael Free from *The Family Book of Best Loved Poems* edited by David L. George. Copyright © 1952 by Doubleday, a division of Bantam Doubleday Dell Publishing Group, Inc.

Ellen Bass for "The Thing Is."

Beacon Press for "Oak Trees of Hope" and "Persistence," from *Guide My Feet* by Marian Wright Edelman. Copyright © 1995 by Marian Wright Edelman. Reprinted by permission of Beacon Press, Boston.

Richard Beban for "Silence."

James Bertolino for "Water's Prayer."

Mike W. Blottenberger for "A Servant's Words."

The Boston Globe Newspaper Company/Washington Post Writers Group for the excerpt "A Wish" by Ellen Goodman. Copyright © 1997. Reprinted with permission.

Noreen Braman for "Wedding Prayer."

Laura Byrnes for "The Cup of Life."

Meg Campbell for "Airborne."

Wave Carberry for "Peace Is Looming."

Chariot Victor Publishing for "Psalm 23 for Busy People" by Toki Miyashina, from *365 Children's Prayers,* edited by Carol Watson, copyright © 1989 by Lion Publishing. Reprinted by permission of Chariot Victor Publishing.

SuzAnne C. Cole for "Living in Hope."

Continuum Publishing Company for "Peace & Unity" by Talamud from *The Gift of Prayer,* by Fellowship in Prayer. Copyright © 1995 by Fellowship in Prayer. Reprinted with permission by The Continuum Publishing Company.

Barbara Crooker for "The Angel of Garage Sales," "Auguries," "In the Middle," and "Prelude."

Phyllis Joy Davison for "Gentle Me, Lord."

William Deerfield for "Loving."

Corrine De Winter for "After the Long Gathering," "God's Way," "Grace," "Now the Heart," and "Sylvan."

Lori Eberhardy for "Angel Embrace."

Susan J. Erickson for "Confiteor" and "Simple Joy."

The Findhorn Press for "Never Be Defeated" by Eileen Caddy from *The Dawn of Change* by Eileen Caddy. Copyright © 1993 by Eileen Caddy. Reprinted by permission of The Findhorn Press, Great Britain.

Suzanne Grosser for "Hope."

Maryanne Hannan for "Epiphany" and "What Forgiveness."

HarperCollins Publishers, Inc. for the excerpt "Every Day" from *Pilgrim at Tinker Creek* by Annie Dillard. Copyright © 1974 by Annie Dillard. Reprinted by permission of HarperCollins Publishers, Inc.

HarperCollins Publishers for "God's World" by Edna St. Vincent Millay from *Collected Poems of Edna St. Vincent Millay.* Copyright © 1956. Reprinted with permission by the Estate of Edna St. Vincent Millay and HarperCollins Publishers.

Permissions and Acknowledgments

198

HarperCollins Publishers, London for "Teach Us to Forgive" by Sheila Cassidy and for "Beatitudes for Disabled People" by Marjorie Chappell from *Laughter, Silence and Shouting* by Kathy Keay. Copyright © 1994. Reprinted by permission of HarperCollins Publishers, London.

Clay Harrison for "Precious Moments."

Harvard University Press for "Hope Is the Thing with Feathers," "It's All I Have to Bring To-Day," "Some Keep the Sabbath Going to Church" and "Time" by Emily Dickinson. Reprinted by permission of the publisher and the Trustees of Amherst College from *The Poems of Emily Dickinson,* Thomas H. Johnson, ed., Cambridge, Mass: The Belknap Press of Harvard University

Press, Copyright © 1951, 1955, 1979, 1983 by the President and Fellows of Harvard University College.

Jill Morgan Hawkins for "Give Us this Day."

C. David Hay for "A Place Remembered" and "Star Wish."

Hazelden Foundation for "Our Real Journey" by Wendell Berry from *Lighting a Candle*, edited by Molly Young Brown. Copyright © 1994 by Hazelden. Reprinted with permission by Hazelden Foundation, Center City, MN.

Rochelle Lynn Holt for "Take Nothing for Granted."

Margaret Anne Huffman for "Open-Hearted Sharing."

International Publishers Co. for the excerpt "It Would Be a Blessing" by Helen Keller from *Helen Keller: Her Socialist Years: Writings and Speeches* edited by Philip S. Foner. Copyright ©1967. Reprinted with permission.

Alfred A. Knopf Inc. for "Dreams" from *Collected Poems* by Langston Hughes. Copyright © 1994 by the Estate of Langston Hughes. Reprinted by permission of Alfred A. Knopf Inc.

Shirley Kobar for "Joy," "Restoration," and "When I'm Weary."

La Alameda Press for "Tulip" by Penny Harter from *Turtle Blessing* by Penny Harter. Copyright © 1996. Reprinted with permission of the author and La Alameda Press.

Elizabeth Searle Lamb for "Letting Go."

Arlene Gay Levine for "The Road."

Liveright Publishing Corporation for the lines from "i thank You God for most this amazing," copyright © 1950, 1978, 1991 by the Trustees for the E. E. Cummings Trust. Copyright © 1979 by George James Firmage, from *Complete Poems: 1904–1962* by E. E. Cummings, edited by George J. Firmage. Reprinted by permission of Liveright Publishing Corporation.

Mary Pat Strenger Loomis for "Heart of Gold."

Louisanna State University Press for "And Then" by Kelly Cherry from *God's Loud Hand: Poems by Kelly Cherry*. Copyright © 1993 by Kelly Cherry. Reprinted with permission by Louisanna State University Press.

Stephen J. Lyons for "Saying Grace."

Renée MacKenzie for "On the Holy Breath of Wind."

Howard McCord for "The Bear that Came to the Wedding."

Many Rivers Press for "Faith" by David Whyte from *Where Many Rivers Meet* by David Whyte. Copyright © 1990 by David Whyte. Reprinted with permission of Many Rivers Press.

Judith Minty for "Deer at the Door."

Joan Noëldechen for "The Inner Flame."

Susan Norton for "Hot Tea Therapy."

Jenifer Nostrand for "Magic."

Julia Older for "Starry Field."

Marian Olson for "Neighbors" and "Woman to Woman."

Thelma J. Palmer for "The Gardener's Toast."

Parallax Press for "The Good News" reprinted from *Call Me By My True Names: The Collected Poems of Thich Nhat Hanh* (1993) by Thich Nhat Hanh with permission of Parallax Press, Berkeley, California.

Random House, Inc. for "Live the Question" and "To Love Another" from *Letters to a Young Poet* by Rainer Maria Rilke, translated by Stephen Mitchell. Copyright © 1984 by Stephen Mitchell. Reprinted by permission of Random House, Inc.

Random House, Inc. for "Miracles" and "I Heard the Learn'd Astronomer Say" by Walt Whitman from *Leaves of Grass* by Walt Whitman. Copyright ©1954 by Random House, Inc.

Riverhead Books, a division of The Putnam Publishing Group for "I Love You, Gentlest of Ways" from *Rilke's Book of Hours* edited by Anita Barrows and Joanna Macy. Copyright ©1996 by Anita Barrows and Joanna Macy. Reprinted by permission of the publisher.

Lora Robertson for "God."

Kate Robinson for "All."

Jo-Anne Rowley for "All Endeavors" and "For the Children."

Hilda Sanderson for "Opportunity" and "Wild Geese."

Rabbi Rami M. Shapiro for "In Forgetting There Is Forgiveness."

Bonita Fogg Smith for "For the Tree Outside My Window."

Jennifer Stanley for "Kneeling to Pick Flowers."

Joan Stephen for "For One in Grief."

Charles E. Tuttle Co., Inc. for "From Within" by Kozan, excerpted from *Japanese Death Poems*, Yoel Hoffman, Copyright © 1986. Published by Charles E. Tuttle Company, Inc., Rutland, Vermont and Tokyo, Japan.

Unity Books for "Healing Hands," "A Healing Prayer" and "There Will Come" from *Today and Every Day* by Elizabeth Searle Lamb, copyright © 1970 by Unity School of Christianity. Used with permission of Unity Books, 1901 NW Blue Parkway, Unity, MO 64065.

Permissions compiled by Tricia Treacy.

Permissions and Acknowledgments

200